HERB DRYING HANDBOOK

P9-BUI-555

HERB DRYING HANDBOOK

Includes Complete Microwave Drying Instructions

Nora Blose and Dawn Cusick

A Sterling/Lark Book
Sterling Publishing Co., Inc.   New York

Photography: Evan Bracken, Light Reflections
Production: Elaine Thompson
Design: Dawn Cusick, Crystal Coates Allen
Illustrations: Crystal Coates Allen
Cover Design: Chris Colando
Contributing Consultant: Sharon Lovejoy

Library of Congress Cataloging-in-Publication Data
Blose, Nora.
   Herb drying handbook : includes complete microwave drying instructions /
Nora Blose and Dawn Cusick.
     p.   c.m.
   "A Sterling/Lark book."
   Includes bibliographical references (p.   ) and indexes.
   ISBN 0-8069-0281-7
   1. Herbs--Drying--Handbooks, manuals, etc.   2. Herbs--Handbooks,
manuals, etc.   3. Herb gardening--Handbooks, manuals, etc.
I. Cusick, Dawn.   II. Title
SB351.H5B55   1993
635'.7—dc20   92–41410
                                                  CIP

10 9 8 7 6 5 4 3

A Sterling/Lark Book

Produced by Altamont Press, Inc.
50 College Street, Asheville, NC 28801 USA

Published in 1993 by Sterling Publishing Co., Inc.
387 Park Avenue South, New York, NY 10016 USA

© 1993, Altamont Press

Distributed in Canada by Sterling Publishing
   c/o Canadian Manda Group, P.O. Box 920, Station U
   Toronto, Ontario, Canada M8Z 5P9
Distributed in the United Kingdom by Cassell PLC
   Villiers House, 41/47 Strand, London WC2N 5JE, England
   P.O. Box 665, Lane Cove, NSW 2066
Distributed in Australia by Capricorn Link Ltd., P.O. Box 665
   Lane Cove, NSW 2066

Every effort has been made to ensure that all information in this book is accurate.
However, due to differing conditions, tools, and individual skills, the publisher
can not be responsible for any injuries, losses, or other damages which may result
from the use of information in this book.

Medicinal information included in this book is not meant to be used for self-
treatment or self-diagnosis. All potentially serious health problems should be
managed by a physician.

Printed in Hong Kong by Pacific Offset
All rights reserved.

ISBN 0-8069-0281-7

Contents

Agrimony, Angelica, Anise Hyssop, Basil, Bay, Bee Balm,
Borage, Broom, Burdock, Calendula, Carnations, Catnip,
Celosia, Chamomile, Chervil, Chicory, Chives, Comfrey,
Coneflower, Coriander, Dill, Dock, Dusty Miller,
Elderberry, Fennel, Feverfew, Garlic, Germander, Heather,
Horehound, Lamb's Ear, Lavender, Lemon Balm, Lemon
Verbena, Lovage, Marjoram, Mint, Mugwort, Parsley,
Pennyroyal, Queen Anne's Lace, Rose, Rosemary, Rue,
Safflower, Sage, Salad Burnet, Santolina, Scented Geranium,
Silver King and Queen Artemisias, Sweet Anise, Sweet
Annie, Tansy, Tarragon, Thyme, and Yarrow

Dedicated in loving memory to my aunt,
Helen Proctor Duggan

N.B.

About the Authors...

Nora Blose lives in the Candler, North Carolina. She became interested in herbs when she lived with her aunt as a child during the depression. Her aunt was the local midwife and country doctor, and Nora spent many childhood days gathering herbs and converting them to medicines. She enjoys growing many of these same herbs today and sharing her knowledge in school and garden club programs. Nora's herbs were recently used to help design one of the sets for *The Last of the Mohicans*.

Photo: Edward Ball

Dawn Cusick lives in Clyde, North Carolina. She is the author of *A Scented Christmas* and *Potpourri Crafts*, and is co-author of *Wreaths 'Round the Year*.

Introduction

If you're like many herb gardeners, you probably find it difficult to say goodbye to the blooms and foliage that you've nurtured and enjoyed throughout the growing season. And while herbs have been preserved with drying techniques since the days of the earliest cultures, many gardeners today quickly become discouraged with the length of time it takes to experiment with drying methods and with the quantity of precious materials that are lost in the learning process.

The Herb Drying Handbook begins with full explanations of six drying methods. More than 60 herbs are then discussed — each one individually — providing you with all the information you need to successfully grow and dry each herb. We've tried to provide you with as many details as possible, hoping they will inspire you to grow and use even more herbs, and to use the wonderful craft of drying to preserve the beauty and fragrance of these ancient plants.

Part I

Harvesting & Drying Techniques

Fortunately, there's nothing mysterious about the process of drying herbs. All you have to do is provide an environment for the herbs' moisture to evaporate and to find a drying method that allows the herbs to retain as much of their natural colors, shapes, and fragrances as possible. As you read through the methods below, try not to be intimidated by what may seem like a series of complicated choices. Every time you dry an herb, even if the results are unsatisfactory, you will become more familiar with the nuances of that particular herb, thus enhancing your relationship with the plants you grow. Part II of this book features profiles of more than 60 individual herbs, giving you an idea of the methods and tips that work best for these herbs. To save you some hassle and disappointment, herbs that do not dry well were not included in the profile section.

Technically, every herb can be dried, but the variations in color and shape are both drastic and subtle, predictable and amazing. Some herbs, no matter which drying method you choose, just shrivel up into an unattractive brown mess. Other herbs retain their bright colors yet lose their distinctive shapes. Others keep their shapes perfectly but shrink so much that you have to dry lots of extra materials. Still others retain their shapes and sizes perfectly but change colors dramatically as they dry, from pink to dark purple, or yellow to brown, for example.

The first step in drying herbs is to harvest them. Because the goal of drying herbs is to rid them of excess moisture, it makes sense to avoid picking the herbs when they're full of moisture, like after a rain shower or when they're covered with early-morning dew. Late morning on a sunny day is often the best choice, after the sun has had a chance to absorb some of the plant's moisture but before the blooms begin to wilt from intense midday heat. Avoid picking materials with damage from insects or mold, and be sure to pick a lot more than you anticipate needing to accommodate shrinkage. If you're harvesting an herb with a culinary use in mind, harvest before the plant blooms, when the flavors tend

to be more intense. Herb blooms should be picked in several stages of growth — from bud form to fully opened — so you can discover which stages hold their color, shape, and size the best.

Once you've chosen a drying method and gotten the drying process underway, be sure to check on the herbs' progress often. Drying times can vary from as little as three or four days to as long as ten weeks, depending on the method and the amount of moisture in the herb when it was harvested. The easiest way to check for dryness is to touch the herbs. The moist vitality that's so enjoyable in fresh-cut herbs will be missing, and they'll feel crisp, like a flake of breakfast cereal. Once your herbs have finished drying, you'll need to find a safe place to store them until you're ready to use them. (Avoid the temptation to keep the herbs hanging or sitting in a desiccant — they'll only overdry and become useless.) Choose a storage location where you won't have to worry about sunlight, insects, or moisture. Cardboard boxes with tight-fitting lids are ideal.

Making a screen drying rack can be as simple or elaborate a project as you desire. For those who don't care about looks, just staple or nail a piece of metal screen to a wood frame and then elevate the screen so there will be air circulation from underneath as well as above. The drying rack pictured here actually serves as a piece of twig furniture, and features several drawers lined with metal screen.

Air-Drying

Most materials can be dried with one of several air-drying techniques. With these methods, the herbs' moisture gently evaporates from the foliage and blooms into the air around them. There are two nice things about this method. Once you've prepared the herbs, you don't have to do anything else. Just stop by every now and then and check on their progress. The other nice thing about air-drying is that it can become a pleasant part of your home's decor if you have a corner in your home that doesn't receive lots of sunlight and isn't exposed to lots of moisture. It also pays to keep an open mind about what makes a nice drying rack or area to hang herb bundles from. Antique yarn spinners, for instance, have nice surface areas to hang herbs from.

Hanging, the oldest of these techniques, involves grouping several stems of the same flower or herb, securing their stems together with string, a clothespin, or a rubber band, and then hanging them upside down in a dark, dry location. The flowers are hung upside down so the blooms will dry in a more natural position. Generally, it makes sense to limit the contents of bundles to one type of herb so their drying times will be the same, and you won't have to break bundles apart when half of the materials are dry and half aren't. If, however, you only have a few materials, very little space, or happen to know that two or three of the herbs have identical drying times, you can mix materials.

Another air-drying method, known as screen or rack drying, involves spreading smaller, single blooms or leaves on a wire screen that has been arranged so there's ventilation on all sides. Prevent excess curling by turning the materials every day or so. With larger blooms, you'll probably want to strip their stems of leaves and then drop the stems through the screen's mesh so that the bottom of the bloom rests flat on the screen for support. Like every other method of drying, completion times will vary, depending on the type of plant and how moist it was when it was harvested. Five to 15 days is an average range.

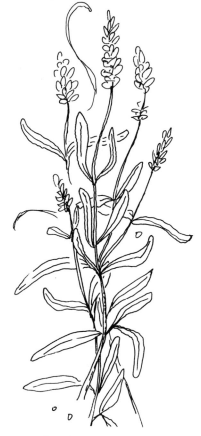

Bundles of air-drying herbs can be hung from just about anything that will support them and provide adequate air circulation. The traditional air-drying rack works well, but so will coat-hangers, rows of string or wire, or even an antique yarn spinner.

Another air-drying option, known as drying-in-place, allows the herbs to dry wherever you place them. You might decide to use this method in several circumstances. If the herb is one that dries particularly well, with no special care, such as yarrow, you can position it in place, such as on a wreath base, and allow it to dry. The other time you might choose this method is if the herb becomes very fragile once dry, and it would be damaged if you tried to attach it to a wreath or other craft project in its dry state. Another time this method makes sense is for herbs like fennel, that will dry in any shape you position them, so you can drape the fennel around the curves of a wreath base, leave it in a dry area, and the fennel will mold itself to the wreath's shape.

Desiccants

Desiccants are moisture-absorbing substances, such as sand, borax, cornmeal, kitty litter, and silica gel. Although several of these desiccants have been used successfully for centuries, they have been superseded in popularity in recent years by silica gel. The negative to most desiccants, though, is that materials dried in them can sometimes reabsorb moisture when exposed to a moist environment such as a kitchen or bathroom, or a rainy, humid part of the country.

Silica gel is the most expensive of these desiccants, but its granules are lighter in weight than those of other desiccants and tend not to crush delicate blooms. Some blooms will only dry in silica gel. Check the progress of your blooms every few days to prevent overdrying, and avoid leaving already-dry blooms in a moist area, such as the bathroom, to prevent the blooms from reabsorbing moisture. Although silica gel may be expensive, it's recyclable so you'll get your investment back fairly soon. The crystals, which tend to be white to pink when purchased, will turn blue when they're full of moisture. This moisture can be removed by spreading the crystals out on a foil-covered baking pan and cooking the crystals in a 200°F (91°C) oven for 20 minutes, or until they change back to their original color.

To dry herb blooms in a desiccant, first sprinkle about an inch (2-1/2 cm) of desiccant on the bottom of a glass or plastic container. (When working with silica gel, be especially careful not to breathe the fumes that will rise up when you pour it. Wearing a mask is a good idea.) Remember that wood and cardboard containers should be avoided because they can allow moisture in. Next, arrange the blooms on top of the desiccant with enough space in between blooms to prevent overlapping. Cup- and bell-shaped blooms should be placed on their sides, while other blooms should be placed face-up. Now sprinkle enough desiccant over the blooms so that all of the petals are covered. With blooms that have multiple rows of petals, you may need to gently pull apart the petals and sprinkle the desiccant in between the petals to ensure even drying. Watch for petals that are bent out of shape and replace them in their normal position. Additional layers of blooms and desiccant can be added if you like.

Gently check your blooms every three days for dryness, using the same criteria as air-drying, and remove them as soon as they're dry. Beware of overdrying: it can remove so much moisture that the blooms will disintegrate when handled. Since desiccant-dried materials can tend to be a bit brittle, handle them carefully, and use a small paint brush to brush away any remaining desiccant.

Novice desiccant dryers should try to limit one type of bloom to a container. Once you've dried a few batches of your favorite blooms and know which ones dry the fastest, you can successfully mix several types of herbs in one container by placing the blooms that take the longest to dry on the bottom and the ones that take the least time to dry on the top layer.

Microwave Drying

The moisture in many varieties of herbs can be removed in just minutes by cooking them in the microwave with silica gel. The process is fairly simple: the microwaves absorb the plant's moisture, and then the silica gel absorbs the moisture to prevent it from being reab-

sorbed by the plant. If you're drying blooms to use in a craft project, such as a wreath or arrangement, then microwave drying is a wonderful option because you can begin working on the craft just 30 minutes after harvesting, compared with one or two weeks if you're using other methods. Because the moisture in flowers can vary so much from variety to variety and even from day to day, and because the wattages in microwaves vary so much, you will need to allow extra flowers and time for experimenting, but once you perfect the times (and make note of them!) you can dry flowers in minutes for the rest of the summer.

As wonderful as microwave drying sounds, there are several times when it's not the ideal method. Microwave drying is not the way to go if you're working with an herb like mint where you intend to use the dried herb in culinary projects. Why? There's no way to dry an herb in the microwave without some of the silica gel's toxicity contaminating the plant. Remember, don't eat anything, not even just a few crumbled basil leaves in a pasta sauce, that's been dried with silica gel. Many culinary herbs can be dried in small quantities in the microwave without silica gel, and these herbs are noted as such in the profiles beginning on page 36. Another time microwave drying isn't ideal is if you're drying for fragrance, because most of the oils in the plant that contain the fragrance are dried up during the cooking process. Luckily, some herbs have unusually strong fragrance oils, which even the microwave can't dry up, and microwave drying is recommended for these herbs in the individual herb profiles. Another time it's not advantageous to use the microwave is when you're drying materials in bulk, such as enough artemisia to make a wreath base. It's far quicker to just make the base with fresh materials and allow the herbs to dry in place than to have to dry eight or nine batches in the microwave.

To dry flowers in the microwave, first add a thin layer of silica gel on the bottom of a microwave-safe container. (If you choose to use a small cardboard box, be sure to check all the corners carefully for staples or metal clips which could damage your oven.) Arrange the flowers in a single layer so their sides don't touch and cover them with another thin layer of silica gel. Microwaves with settings from 1 through 10 should be put on setting number 4 (about 300 watts); a microwave with three or four settings should be put on "half" power (about 350 watts); and a microwave with "high" and "defrost" settings should be put on "defrost (about 200 watts). Begin with two-and-a-half minutes and allow a standing time of ten minutes. If your flowers overdried, start again with fresh materials and reduce the time in 30-second intervals. If the flowers are still not dry, add time in 15-second intervals.

Pressing

This method is one of the simplest and oldest techniques for preserving herbs. You can press your flowers in something as simple as between the pages of a large dictionary or with something as elaborate as a 20-tier flower press. To press your herbs, begin by removing the foliage and blooms from the stems. Arrange them on a sheet of blotting paper, allowing enough space between each material to prevent overlapping. Check first for creases and folds in the petals and leaves, and then cover them with another sheet of blotting paper. Now place the herbs between the pages of a thick book or a flower press. They should be completely dry in six to ten weeks.

Basic Craft Tools

Floral Picks are actually small wooden picks with short lengths of fine-gauge wire attached. They are used to secure stems of flowers or foliage that are too weak to insert directly into a foam or straw base. The end of the pick is precut at an angle to make perforation into the base easier. Floral picks can also be used as a time-saving device: Instead of picking one stem into a base at a time, you can attach small bouquets of materials to a single pick. There's no set rule about how many stems should be in each bouquet. Three to five is a good guideline, but some materials may have such thin stems that you can pick eight or nine together, while others may be so thick that you'll have difficulty attaching two stems to a floral pick.

To use a floral pick, position the pick against the stem(s) so the pick extends about 1 inch (2-1/2 cm) below the stems. Wrap the wire around the stems twice in the same place, then wrap and spiral the wire down around the stems and the pick to bind them together. Trim the stems where the wire ends. If the stems are especially fragile, you can add strength by wrapping the picked stems with floral tape.

Floral Pins are U-shaped pieces of wire look and work like old-fashioned hairpins. Purchase the pins in a color (green and silver are available) that will blend in with your materials. To use a floral pin, simply position the materials you're attaching against a straw or foam base, position the pin with its prongs on either side of the material, and press the pin into the base at an angle.

Floral Tape comes in several shades of brown and green that are compatible with natural materials. Floral tape is most often used to add strength to a floral pick that's holding multiple, delicate stems. The only trick to success with floral tape is to stretch it gently as you're working with it to increase its adhesive quality.

Floral Wire is one of those inexpensive, invaluable tools every crafter should have around the house. It's available in a variety of different thicknesses (referred to as gauge), in several different colors (brown, green, and silver), and is sold in pre-cut lengths and on spools. Thin and medium gauges of wire tend to be more flexible and thus easier to work with, although the thicker gauges can add some much-needed strength if you're trying to attach an unusually heavy item to a base. Always choose the color that will blend in best with the materials you're wiring. Short lengths of floral wire are used to attach single items, such as bows, to wreath bases, whereas wire in spool-form is used to attach small bouquets of dried or artificial flowers to single wire wreath bases.

To attach materials to a wire base, first cut the stems of the materials to a consistent length. Four-inch (10 cm) lengths work well with the standard 10- to 12-inch-diameter (25 to 30 cm) wire ring bases; for smaller bases, trim the materials to 2-1/2 or 3 inches (6 to 7 cm) in length; for larger bases, trim the materials to 5 or 6 inches (12 to 15 cm) in length. Arrange the materials into small bouquets of three to five stems per bouquet.

Position the first bouquet against the wire ring base and attach it by wrapping the spool wire around the stems of the materials and the base several times. Do not cut the spool wire. Position the next bouquet so its flowers or greenery overlap the wired stems of the previous bouquet and wrap several times with floral wire. Continue in this way until the entire base is covered. You can decide that your wreath is finished at this point or hot-glue single blooms onto the wired materials.

Page 31

Bunches of fresh-cut sage were picked into a straw base to form the wreath's background, and coneflower blooms were then hot-glued into the sage as colorful accents.

Page 32

Top Potpourri: This potpourri is pretty to look at and also makes a soothing bath mix. It contains bee balm blooms, rose petals, lavender, peppermint, comfrey, lemon verbena, and chamomile.

Bottom Potpourri: This potpourri uses the historical symbolic meanings of plants to create a potpourri to encourage sweet dreams. The potpourri contains peppermint, spearmint, rosemary, lemon balm, honesty, and roses.

Part II

•

Herb
Profiles

•

Monarda, Chives
& Sage

Agrimony

Also known as dog burr plant, this 3- to 5-foot (.9 to 1.5 m) perennial grows easily in full sun and dappled shade, and is often found growing wild in fields and along roadsides. It needs very little care, and self-sows itself in large numbers. In the mid-1600s, Culpepper's *Color Herbal* described agrimony as being "good against the biting and stinging of serpents." Agrimony has also been used by several native cultures as a natural dye, and today many herbalists recommend mixing it with witch hazel to form a refreshing astringent.

Drying

Agrimony should be harvested after it has flowered. The fresh-cut spikes can be hung upside down in small bundles, arranged on a screen, or preserved in silica gel. (If you choose to hang dry the spikes, do not separate the bundles after drying unless you're prepared for a lot of shattering.) Pressing agrimony leaves showcases their lovely shape and interesting texture. The bright green leaves fade to an olive green as they dry and lose about 30% of their size.

Crafts

Agrimony leaves can be used in just about any dried craft project that needs some greenery, though it's not an ideal material for crafts that may get bumped against because it's fairly fragile. The burr-like bloom spikes provide an intriguing contrast to traditional flower shapes in wreaths, garlands, and arrangements.

The seeds provide children who have pets with a fun nature lesson, illustrating perfectly how easily seeds are dispersed when they attach to an animal's fur and fall off somewhere down the road in the animal's travels.

Angelica

A tall biennial averaging 6 to 8 feet (1.8 to 2.4 m), angelica thrives with little care in partial shade and rich, quick-draining soil. The shiny green foliage is decorated with small, simple white blooms, and the plant radiates a delicate, licorice-like fragrance. The name angelica is said to derive from its angelic healing ability, and people carried it to ward off witches.

Drying

The foliage can be harvested at any time during the growth cycle, while the flower heads should be harvested at the peak of their bloom. The flower heads dry well when hung upside down in small bundles or arranged on a screen rack, although the foliage tends to curl with these two methods. Pressing also works well. The leaves curl a little as they dry, while the flower heads retain their shape and remain sturdy. A little of the licorice fragrance remains after drying.

Cuisines and Crafts

Angelica seeds add a licorice flavor to teas and baked goods. The stems and leaves can be crystallized by cutting the stems and leaves into 5-inch (13 cm) pieces and layering them in a long glass bowl. Next, make a crystallizing syrup by bringing one part sugar to two parts water to a boil. Pour the syrup over the stems and leaves and allow them to cool for 24 hours. The next day, put the coated angelica back in the saucepan and heat slowly to a boil. Simmer until the stems and leaves turn a bright green. Drain, cool, and garnish with a layer of fine sugar.

The flower heads and blooms are ideal for larger, showy herbal wreaths, as well as larger garlands and pressed pictures.

Monarda, Chives & Sage

Carnations, Bay
& Lavender

Anise Hyssop

A tender perennial, anise hyssop enjoys much of its popularity because of a pungent fragrance that's amazingly similar to licorice (thus the common nickname fennel hyssop), and seems to attract bees (thus another common nickname, bee plant). Anise hyssop averages 2 to 4 feet in height (61 cm to 1.2 m), and flourishes in partial sun and well-drained soil. Anise hyssop will come back every spring if your winters aren't too severe and the old stems are cut off in the fall, and the herb also reseeds itself from the flower heads. The tall, lavender flower spikes look pretty scattered throughout an herb garden and make an especially nice color complement when planted near herbs with bright yellow flowers.

Drying

Harvest the flower stalks when the colors are in full bloom. Hang them upside down in a dry, dark place or upright in a vase. Flower stalks picked very early in the bloom cycle can also be dried by pressing. The blooms shrink very little, maintain most of their color and licorice-like fragrance, and are relatively sturdy as long as you handle them gently.

Cuisines and Crafts

Anise hyssop blooms can be used to add flavor and color to salads, pastas, dressings, oils, potatoes, teas, and vinegars.

The blooms add color, fragrance, and interesting shapes to wreaths, arrangements, garden hats, and bouquets. Whole blooms can also be crumbled and added to herbal potpourris.

Basil

Carnations, Bay & Lavender

Beloved by chefs and food connoisseurs alike, this flavorful, fragrant annual attracts bees and likes to be pinched back frequently. The essential oil in basil actually contains camphor, and many herbalists believe a basil infusion can ease stomach pains. In 1649, long before basil was recognized as a culinary herb, Culpepper reported the following information in his *Color Herbal.* "This is the herb which all authors are together by the ears about, and rail at one another, like lawyers. Galen and Dioscorides hold it not fitting to be taken inwardly, and Chrysippus rails at it with downright Billingsgate rhetoric: Pliny and the Arabian physicians defend it."

Drying

Basil leaves should be harvested before the plant blooms. Unless you live in a very humid environment, the leaves will dry well by hanging the stems upside down in small bunches. Screen drying also works if you turn the leaves frequently, as well as microwaving on some paper towels without silica gel for about a minute. The leaves will shrink by about 50%, become much more fragile, and turn to a brownish/white color if they're from sweet basil plants and to a purplish/brown if they're from a dark opal plant. Basil blooms usually lose their tiny florets as they dry, although they maintain their interesting shape well and are relatively sturdy.

Cuisines and Crafts

Basil leaves can be used to flavor eggs, tomatoes, and pasta sauces, to name just a few of the possibilities. Leaves dried from a summer garden should be crumbled into a small bowl of olive oil or white wine and stirred occasionally for several hours before using. The leaves and blooms from the dark opal basil are a little too tart for some tastes, although their lovely color makes a beautiful homemade vinegar.

If you have enough of it, basil makes a nice material for wreath background. Just attach fresh-cut stems to a straw base with floral pins and then hang the wreath in a dry, dark place until it's dry. The wreath will emanate a light fragrance that is very pleasurable if you like basil.

Roses, Lamb's Ears, & Scented Geraniums

Bay

This tender perennial has been revered through the centuries for a variety of reasons. Herbalists in the 1600s believed that ingesting bay encouraged a speedy childbirth. Bay is revered today for its peppery fragrance and flavor. If you've only seen bay leaves in the spice department of the grocery store, you'd find the 20-foot (m) bay trees common in warm winter climates nothing less than amazing. In colder climates bay is a tender perennial and needs to be brought indoors for the winter. Bay trees need little care, although they do enjoy rich soil with mulch, a top dressing once or twice a year, and a good fertilizing with fish emulsion every few months.

Drying

Harvest the leaves at any time if you live in a warm-winter climate; otherwise, harvest them in the summer months. The leaves can be dried individually on a screen rack or hung upside down in small bunches. The leaves also press well. The leathery, dark green leaves lighten a little as they dry. They don't curl, shrink very little, and are fairly sturdy.

Cuisines and Crafts

Bay leaves are frequently called for in soup, stew, sauce, and vinegar recipes. Bay is an integral ingredient to the traditional bouquet garnis made from three parsley sprigs, one bay leaf, and one sprig of thyme, all tied together with string. A single bay leaf placed in cereal and flour packages discourages the presence of small, intrusive bugs.

Bay leaves are a popular material in herbal crafts for several reasons. Their culinary associations make them the ideal background material for kitchen wreaths accented with garlic bulbs, yellow yarrow, and spices like cinnamon sticks and star anise. Individual bay leaves can be hot-glued in position, or several stems of leaves can be attached to a floral pick and inserted into a straw, foam, or vine base. Bay leaves also make nice additions to decorative and fragrant potpourris, as well as moth and flea repellent potpourris. Bay swags can be made by stringing bay leaves and fruits on heavy string with a tapestry needle.

Bee Balm

Bee Balm, also known as horse mint and bee mint, is a favorite of bees. It thrives in full sun to partial shade, likes well-drained soil, and grows to 2 to 3 feet (61 to 91 cm) tall. This herb is a favorite of gardeners because the bright blooms invite bees, hummingbirds, and butterflies.

Drying

Harvest bee balm blooms just after they've opened, and be sure to leave some for the birds. It dries well by hanging the stems upside down in small bunches. Expect the leaves to shrink to about 50% of their fresh size, so cut extra if you're planning to make a wreath. The bright blooms retain most of their color as they dry, as does the foliage. The blooms maintain their shape fairly well; the leaves tend to curl as they dry, although they retain much of their fresh, minty fragrance.

Cuisines and Crafts

The blooms can be steeped in boiling water for a gentle, minty tea.

In crafts, the bright blooms add color to potpourris, arrangements, wreaths, topiaries, and much more. Stems of fresh-cut bee balm can also be positioned around a metal ring wreath base, secured with monofilament, and left to dry in a dark room to create a fragrant, colorful wreath. The blooms are exquisite when individual florets are used in pressed flower pictures or on the outsides of candles.

Roses, Lamb's Ears, & Scented Geraniums

Monarda, Chives & Sage

Betony

This carefree perennial spreads well and attracts bees. It averages 2 to 3 feet (61 to 91 cm), and likes both full sun and partial shade. A member of the mint family and native to Europe and Asia Minor, betony radiates a very delicate, light mint fragrance. Anciently known as woundwort, the herb was an important medicinal herb in the middle ages and Elizabethan times, being used for the eyes, bladder, and "joynts."

Drying

Harvest the leaves just as the plant begins to flower; harvest the bloom spikes at their peak. Hanging upside down in small bundles works fine for the foliage, although the leaves will shatter if you try to separate the bundles after they've finished drying. The leaves and blooms also dry well when arranged on a screen rack or pressed. The leaves fade to a light green as they dry and shrink to about 70% of their fresh-cut size, while the blooms retain their bright color well if dried carefully.

Cuisines and Crafts

Betony leaves make an exotic homemade herbal tea when mixed with mint and lemon verbena. The bright-colored flowers taste very sweet and make a nice addition to sherbets, ice creams, and fruit salads.

Borage

Centuries ago, many people believed that borage could "expel pensiveness and melancholy," and while that may not be a belief held by the modern medical community, any herbal gardener can attest to the uplifting results of just looking at borage's delicate, star-shaped lavender/blue blooms. Although it's an annual, you probably will never have to re-plant it because borage self-seeds very well.

Drying

The leaves can be harvested at any time during the growth cycle, while the flowers should be harvested just past their peak for best results. The blooms dry fairly well when arranged face-down on a screen rack, although the best color retention occurs when they're preserved in silica gel. (Hanging upside down to air-dry in small bundles tends to produce mediocre results.) The blooms also press beautifully. The leaves and blooms shrink a lot as they dry and tend to be very delicate.

Cuisines and Crafts

As long as you haven't dried them in silica gel, borage blooms can bring herbal beauty to lots of recipes. Try floating individual blooms on top of mixed drinks, punches, and chilled soups, or use them to garnish a fruit salad. The blooms can also be used to decorate cream cheeses and tea sandwiches. For a special gift, crystallize the blooms and gently layer them in a crystal bottle.

Single borage blooms can be used to decorate candles, picture frames, bookmarks, and stationery, or to accent wreaths and garlands.

Monarda, Chives & Sage

Carnations, Bay & Lavender

Broom

Also known as Scotch broom, this 6- to 7-foot (1.8 to 2.1 m) shrub needs little care and spreads like a weed. Scotch broom is native to Old World countries, while other members of this large species are native to Europe, the Canary Islands, North Africa, and Eastern Asia.

Drying

The foliage can be harvested at any time of the growth cycle, while the blooms should be picked at their peak. The foliage dries well on screens or by hanging upside down in small bundles. The blooms look best when pressed or dried in silica gel. The foliage retains its dark green color, curls just a little, and doesn't shrink in size. The blooms retain their bright yellow color but tend to be fragile.

Crafts

The foliage makes a good background material for wreaths, garlands, and door swags. The pressed blooms look remarkably like a hummingbird in flight, making them ideal decorations for pressed pictures, candles, and stationery.

To make a broom similar to those the Indians made from this herb, gather several long branches and bind them together at the stems with twine. The twiggy ends form the "broom", and it makes a good tool for sweeping dirt from garden pathways.

Burdock

Also known by such intriguing common names as beggar burr, dog burr, and turkey burr, this 3- to 6-foot (.9 to 1.8 m) biennial is native to Europe and Asia, and is frequently found growing wild along roadsides in America. It will tolerate conditions ranging from dry to wet and sunny to shady.

Culpepper's famous *Color Herbal*, published in 1649, reports that "the root beaten with a little salt and laid on the place bitten by a snake will suddenly easeth the pain." Although this herb is harvested primarily for its burr stalks, the plant's tiny red blooms make it an attractive addition to the garden.

Drying

Harvest the burrs after they've finished flowering, and arrange them on a screen rack to dry. Don't expect any changes in size, shape, or coloring: dried burdock burrs look almost identical to fresh-cut burrs.

Crafts

Burr stalks make interesting additions to wreaths, arrangements, bouquets, and garlands. The individual burrs are virtually indestructible, and they make wonderful nature toys for children because they can be stuck together like building blocks to form animals, houses, and almost anything else a child's imagination can invent. *Sunflower Houses* (Interweave Press, 1992), a book of children's garden stories, mentions a tale from the 1800s about children who made burr baskets by cutting the burrs in half and filling them with miniature flowers. The burrs can also be arranged in a border around tender plants to protect them from slugs.

Carnations, Bay & Lavender

Roses, Lamb's Ears, & Scented Geraniums

Calendula

Calendula's bright, golden yellow and orange blooms have inspired several charming common names over the years, including Mary's gold, pot marigold, and Miss morning. For centuries calendula has been revered for its reputed abilities to soothe the skin, and several creams are marketed with calendula oil in them. It can grow as tall as 2 feet (61 cm), and seems to thrive in hot weather and dry, exposed areas that often wilt other flowers. About the only thing calendula can't tolerate is waterlogged roots. In most areas calendula is an annual, although in the warm climates it lives year 'round.

Drying

Calendula is a popular herb to dry because the bright blooms retain virtually all of their color, shape, and strength. The leaves curl slightly as they dry, but have a pleasing shape and color. Harvest calendula after the blooms have opened. You can hang calendula upside down to dry in small bunches, but the petals tend to curl and you may be unhappy with the results. Single blooms dry well on a screen rack when placed face down. Microwave drying also works well. Calendula blooms tend to be too thick to press well, although individual petals can be removed from the blooms and pressed separately with beautiful results.

Cuisines and Crafts

Individual calendula petals can be added to soft cheeses, butters, omelettes, salads, yogurts, cakes, and sweet breads for a tangy flavor. The petals also work beautifully in pasta prima flora and in rice dishes as a substitute for saffron.

Bright calendula blooms add a burst of color to potpourris and wreaths, and arrangements. Stems can be created for the blooms with floral wire and tape, or you can simply hot-glue the single flower heads in place. Small sachet bags can be filled with crushed blooms and foliage and then tied around your bath spout to infuse the bath water with calendula's skin-soothing oils.

Carnations

Carnations have been a favorite of gardeners for centuries, and it's difficult to tell whether the attraction originates with the delicate blooms or the gray-blue foliage. While pink is the most common color, carnations also come in shades of peach, cream, white, and red. Dead blooms should be pinched off as soon as possible and the plants should be sheared down when they've finished blooming for the season. This perennial likes full sun and well-drained soil, and the plants will spread into a beautiful mat of gray-blue foliage as the years pass.

Drying

For the best results, carnation blooms should be harvested on the first day they open. The blooms and leaves can be dried separately on a screen rack or in a desiccant. The blooms tend to close up a bit while the leaf edges curl slightly. The leaves and blooms press well, and microwave drying with silica gel also works.

Cuisines and Crafts

Carnation petals are a time-tested culinary delicacy. Try sprinkling a few petals in your next fruit salad or into a champagne punch. The petals can also be mixed into jellies, sorbets, rose syrups, and even vinegars.

Dried carnation blooms look lovely in wreaths, especially those with backgrounds made from moss, sweet Annie, or 'Silver King' artemisia. The blooms also look nice in potpourris. Pressed blooms and leaves can be used to decorate note papers, picture frames, and photo albums.

Roses, Lamb's Ears, & Scented Geraniums

Monarda, Chives
& Sage

Catnip

Named for its ability to lure and charm felines, catnip is a fast-spreading perennial that can grow up to 3 feet (91 cm) in height and thrives in just about any variety of soil. Also known as cat's toy and cat's play, the plant attracts bees in addition to cats.

Drying

The blooms and foliage shrink at least 50% during the drying process. The leaves curl a little and darken, while the blooms shrivel up and lose most of their lavender coloring. The fresh, woodsy fragrance remains after drying. Harvest the leaves when they're young, and harvest the blooms after they're fully open but before they begin to turn brown. Dry your catnip by hanging it upside down in small bunches or by microwaving it for about 1-1/2 minutes.

Cuisines and Crafts

Catnip leaves can be steeped in boiling water for a pleasant tea that early herbalists believed could soothe colic, upset stomachs, and headaches. Catnip leaves can also be rubbed onto raw meat as a tenderizer or mixed with olive oil and seasonings for a marinade..

Although dried catnip foliage is very attractive, it can be crumbled and used for its fragrance in potpourris, sleep pillows, and sachets. If you have a feline in the house, though, be kind and don't tempt them beyond their ability to restrain themselves.

Celosia

Celosia

Both the plumed and crested varieties of celosia are a popular annual plant choice for many gardeners and dried flower crafters, although some herb connoisseurs find it lacking in the qualities that make herbs seem so magical. They are easy to grow from seed, tend to be pest free, and can tolerate neglect as long as they receive enough water.

Drying

Celosia should be harvested at the peak of its flowering cycle. Hang the blooms upside down to dry in small bundles or arrange them on a screen rack. Expect the brilliant colors to fade just a little and to shrink about 10 to 20% in size. The blooms of both varieties are very sturdy when dry, and can be used whole or separated into smaller pieces.

Crafts

Plumed celosia blooms look lovely in potpourris when they've been separated into smaller florets. Crested celosia, also known as cockscomb, makes a nice embellishment for the tops of glass tree ornaments. Both varieties are often chosen for wreaths, garlands, swags, arrangements, and many other dried craft projects because of their bright colors. The burgundy crested celosia makes an ideal choice for Christmas crafts. Celosia florets also add a splash of color to display potpourris that smell wonderful but aren't very attractive to look at.

Monarda, Chives & Sage

Carnations, Bay & Lavender

Chamomile

Also known as the plant's doctor, chamomile has been a versatile herb both in the garden and in cuisines and crafts for a long time. Chamomile can be enjoyed in the garden as a small accent plant or arranged in small plugs about 10 inches (25 cm) apart to create a lawn that looks like it's been carpeted in chamomile. Although it will need a daily watering when first planted this way, the chamomile will soon be strong enough to tolerate moderate foot traffic.

Drying

Chamomile flowers should be harvested when they are fully opened, while the foliage can be harvested at any time. Chamomile can be dried with upright or hang drying, screens, or pressing. Chamomile's golden yellow and white blooms retain most of their color and shape, and retain their delicate, apple-like scent after they've dried.

Cuisines and Crafts

Chamomile may be best savored as a hot tea. Just steep fresh or dried blooms for a few minutes in water that's been brought to a gentle roll. Many people find that just smelling the tea can reduce stress, and it tastes great too!

Chamomile's small blooms look lovely in potpourris, garlands, and wreaths. Though too fragile for most craft uses, the leaves can be used to add fragrance to sachets and dream pillows.

Chervil

Centuries ago, herbal doctors recommended boiled chervil roots be eaten with oil and vinegar to ease stomach and lung problems. This hardy annual likes full sun to partial shade, lots of water, and does not transplant well. In hot weather it often goes to seed so early in the season that you will get a second crop. It averages 10 inches (25 cm) in height and doesn't mind being planted in clusters.

Drying

The leaves should be harvested just before the plant blooms, and the flowers should be harvested before they begin to fade. Screen drying, hanging, pressing, and microwaving all work well. The pale green leaves develop a golden tinge and curl slightly as they dry, while the tiny white or cream blooms, although delicate, retain their color well.

Cuisines and Crafts

Chervil's unique flavor is sometimes described as a cross between parsley and anise, and once you taste the difference it can make in your everyday recipes you won't want to cook without it. The leaves can be steeped in boiling water for a refreshing tea, or added at the end of the cooking time to soups, sauces, and recipes featuring chicken, fish, or eggs. The leaves can also be mixed in with dinner salads.

Chervil's small flowers add an airy feel to wreaths, garlands, and swags. The leaves can be used to decorate candles, photo albums, stationery, and picture frames.

Carnations, Bay & Lavender

Roses, Lamb's Ears, & Scented Geraniums

Chicory

Also known as succory, this hardy perennial averages 3 to 5 feet (.9 to 1.5 m) and thrives in sunny, open areas. Centuries ago, Dioscorides recommended, "Drink twice or thrice a day with wine to bring immunity in pestilential seasons." Today, chicory is grown primarily for culinary reasons, although some people find the taste a little too bitter.

Drying

Harvest the leaves when they're young, dig the roots in the autumn, and harvest the flowers before they peak. Dry the leaves, flowers, and roots by hanging them upside down in small bundles. The roots and individual flowers also dry well on a screen rack.

Cuisines

The flowers can be sprinkled over salads or pickled. Roasted chicory roots can be steeped in boiling water to form a coffee-like drink. The roots can be boiled and served with a light sauce or blanched and served in salads. To make a beautiful autumn vinegar, fill a decanter with the flowers and cover them with vinegar. Allow the flavor and color to infuse the vinegar for a few weeks and then enjoy.

Chives

This member of the onion family was once believed to have "sent up very hurtful vapors to the brain, causing troublesome sleep and spoiling the eyesight." Thank goodness the rumors turned out false. Today, this perennial is grown and harvested for its pungent flavor and lively purple blooms. Chive plants attract bees and grow well in full sun and rich soil. They also spread well, making them an ideal border for culinary gardens.

Drying

The purple-mauve blooms retain virtually all of their size and color. The dried blooms are sturdy and the stems are supple and may lose their color as they dry. Compared to fresh-cut chives, the odor is about 50% as pungent in the dried blooms, although some people may still find it too strong to enjoy in indoor crafts. The blooms should be harvested immediately after they open to prevent them from crumbling. The stems can be harvested at any time, and the bulbs should be harvested in late autumn or early spring. The blooms and stems dry well on a rack, hung upside down, or in the microwave for about a minute. Individual florets can be separated from the bloom and pressed with lovely results.

Cuisines and Crafts

Chive stems can be diced and mixed with butters, cream cheeses, and soups. To make an unusual but flavorful salad, top each serving with a chive blossom for color and flavor. Individual florets separated from the blooms also work well in spice blends, and a whole bloom adds just the right touch to homemade herbal vinegars, oils, and wines.

Chive blooms make wonderful accents in potpourris and wreaths, and they're an ideal choice because they look delicate but are actually quite sturdy and also retain their colors very well over the years. Because their stems are so weak, you will need to rely on a glue gun to attach the blooms.

Roses, Lamb's Ears, & Scented Geraniums

Monarda, Chives
& Sage

Comfrey

Known by such common names as all-heal, healer, knitbone, and bruisewort, it's no accident that comfrey shares the same root word as comfortable and comfort. Early herbals reported that comfrey's roots could be boiled in water or wine to heal interior bruises and wounds. Today, comfrey leaves are made into ointments and salves for external wounds.

A determined perennial, comfrey plants are usually strong and healthy, needing little care once they get started. The plants attract lots of bees, and grow best in full or partial sun and when treated to a top mulching in the spring. Comfrey makes a good plant to share with fellow herb enthusiasts because just a small piece of root will produce a plant. It also makes a productive contribution to compost heaps.

Drying

Comfrey's purple/rose or white blooms should be harvested just before or just as they flower, and the leaves should be harvested in the summer. The blooms and leaves both dry well when hung upside down in small bundles or arranged on a screen rack. Because the leaves contain an unusually high amount of moisture, it helps if they're dried in a warmer-than-usual location, such as near a water heater or in an attic. Expect the leaves to turn a darker green, shrink a lot, and become quite brittle as they dry. The grassy, earth-like fragrance remains fairly strong.

Cuisines and Crafts

Although many contemporary herbalists recommend comfrey tea for healing purposes, there is some concern among medical researchers about comfrey's safety when ingested.

Single comfrey blooms can be hot-glued into wreaths, garlands, swags, and many other crafts. Comfrey's healing qualities can be enjoyed externally by mixing crushed leaves into homemade soaps and bath sachets.

Coneflower

Large, bright purple coneflowers are the glory of many an herb garden, attracting the attention of bees, butterflies, skippers, and frequent passersby. They grow well in full sun and in just about any soil. A 3- to 4-foot (91 cm to 1.2 m) perennial, coneflowers need little care and will spread slowly but surely once they're established.

Drying

Coneflowers should be harvested at the peak of their blooming cycle, before the petals begin to fall from the center. They can be hung upside down to dry in single stems (as opposed to the small bunches of stems usually used with this method) or placed flat on a screen rack. The blooms can also be preserved in silica gel, or the petals can be removed and pressed individually. Color retention is best with silica gel, although it's fairly good with the other methods.

Crafts

Coneflower blooms add a splash of color to wreaths, arrangements, garlands, and many other craft projects. Length and strength can be added to their stems by holding a piece of floral wire against a stem and securing the two together with floral tape. The individual blooms can also be hot-glued in place or simply arranged on top of a potpourri recipe. Although sometimes overshadowed by the blooms, the orange-tinged seed heads are also attractive in many crafts.

Monarda, Chives & Sage

Carnations, Bay & Lavender

Coriander

Also known as cilantro and Mexican parsley, this annual herb is well known for its flavoring abilities. The plant averages one to two feet (61 cm) in height, and likes full sun and well-drained soil. Coriander self sows prolifically and is a favorite of bees. The foliage is a lovely green, while the blooms feature tiny white flowers with tinges of lavender and pale pink.

Drying

Coriander can be harvested at any time of the growth cycle. It is very delicate and tends to droop no matter which drying method you choose. For craft use, pressing is by far the best way to preserve the beauty of the blooms and foliage. For culinary use, hanging tends to produce the best results. The seeds can be gathered by placing a small paper bag over each bouquet, attaching it with a rubber band, and hanging them upside down to dry as you normally would. Remove the fallen seed from the bags after the coriander has dried. (You can dry the coriander on a screen, but then you have to rescue the fallen seed from the floor.) Harvest more coriander than you anticipate needing to make up for the substantial shrinkage that occurs during drying.

Cuisines and Crafts

For a wonderful homemade salsa, mix 10 sliced tomatoes, 1 finely chopped onion, 1/2 finely chopped red pepper, and 20 to 30 chopped coriander leaves. Stir all of the ingredients together and allow them to marinate in the refrigerator for 12 hours before serving. Coriander is also used to flavor chutneys and curries, and can even be used to add a hint of spice to apple pie. If using in a soup or other recipe that will be cooked, use the stems and the leaves; if the food will not be cooked, do not use the stems.

Coriander's blooms do not dry well and the leaves are very delicate, so this herb is rarely used in wreaths or arrangements. The seeds, however, make a nice contribution to potpourris and simmering spices. For fresh bouquets, coriander is a knock-out. Pressed foliage and blooms can be used to decorate note papers or the outside of candles.

Dill

Also known as lull plant and door dill, this annual herb was grown in the 1600s to ease pains and encourage sleep. Today, however, dill is grown for its culinary pleasures. It re-seeds itself every year and needs very little care, thriving in full sun and well-drained soil. Dill's only peccadillo is that it doesn't transplant well.

Drying

If you plan to use the foliage for cooking, harvest it before the plant blooms. The foliage can be dried by hanging upside down in small bundles, on screen racks, or in the microwave without silica gel for about a minute. Individual flower heads dry best on screens or with the pressing method, although you can also hang them upside down to dry with the foliage. The seeds can be collected easily by tying small paper bags over the flowers before hanging them.

The feathery foliage turns to an olive green color as it dries and becomes quite fragile. The blooms turn to a light gold and remain relatively sturdy, although they will curl up unless they're picked at their peak. Dill also retains much of its fragrance after drying.

Cuisines and Crafts

Almost everyone's heard of dill pickles, but dill is so much more versatile. The seeds can be used to flavor breads, vinegars, or cabbage, and much more. The foliage makes a wonderful salt substitute for eggs, potatoes, sauces, soups, stews, as well as an attractive garnish.

Dill blooms are attractive in just about any dried herb craft — wreaths, garlands, soaps, and even potpourris. Although quite delicate, the foliage adds a lovely, willowy look to craft projects.

Carnations, Bay & Lavender

Roses, Lamb's Ears, & Scented Geraniums

Dock

Also known as Indian tobacco, wild sorrel, wayside dock, and bloodwort, this 2- to 4-foot (.6 to 1.2 m) perennial has been used for lots of different purposes over the centuries. The roots were often boiled to form a bath to soothe skin itches and sores, and the seeds were once used in place of coffee.

Think long and hard before you decide to plant dock in your home garden because it can literally take over your yard. (This is a good herb to plant in your neighbor's rose bed in the dead of night if his dog has messed in your garden one too many times.) Instead, gather it from roadsides or disturbed, wet areas.

Drying

Harvest the magenta blooms before they begin to darken and shed; harvest the seeds after the plant has bloomed and the seeds have had a chance to form; harvest the leaves when they're young. Dry the blooms and seeds upside down in small bundles. Dry the leaves on a screen rack. The blooms, seed heads, and leaves all press well.

Crafts

Although the blooms and leaves can be used in many craft projects, it's the seed heads that are valued for the attractive contrast they provide in wreaths, swags, garlands, and arrangements. The lovely autumn colors in dried dock make it an especially nice choice for harvest season crafts.

Dusty Miller

This Mediterranean plant loves sunshine so much that it will desperately contort itself to get the maximum sun exposure. (If you plant it on a shady bank, for instance, it will grow lopsided to reach the sun.) The foliage is beautiful to look at — a rich gray with silver and green highlights and a stunning shape — making it a lovely choice for borders and all-gray gardens. Dusty miller ranges from 1 to 2-1/2 feet (30 to 76 cm) in height and is a hardy perennial. It requires little care, although you may need to thin it once a year to prevent the roots from molding.

Drying

Dusty miller leaves shrink very little and maintain their silvery color. Individual leaves can be harvested at any stage of growth and then placed on a screen rack to dry. The bright yellow bloom clusters also retain their color and shape: just tie them in small bundles and hang them upside down to dry.

Crafts

The leaves and blooms add beautiful shape and color to pot-pourris. They're also a wonderful choice for decorating smaller items such as Christmas ornaments. To make an herbal Christmas ornament, hot-glue a leaf down each side of a glass ball; then hot-glue several smaller herb blooms, such as dried rose buds, where the stems meet and add some narrow satin ribbon loops if desired. (Note: You may find it easier to glue the leaf to the ornament when it's fresh-picked and allow it to dry in place.) Dusty miller also looks lovely in arrangements and wreaths, although you may prefer to work with it fresh-picked and let it dry in place if you'll be curving it around a base or other material.

Roses, Lamb's Ears, & Scented Geraniums

Monarda, Chíves & Sage

Elderberry

Also known as flute tree and music tree, the elderberry tree can grow as tall as 40 feet (1.2 km) in very warm climates. (It averages between 5 and 15 feet (1.5 to 4.5 m) in climates with colder winters.) Although it loves moisture, elderberries seem to be able to survive the harshest conditions. The tree attracts lots of birds when it's in fruit, so plant it near a window if you can.

Drying

Harvest the dark green foliage and the creamy white flowers during the peak of bloom; harvest the berries in late autumn. Air-drying with a screen rack and hanging works well for foliage, flowers, and berries; the blooms also dry well with desiccants and with pressing. The dried foliage curls a little but remains sturdy; the blooms take on a brownish tinge and maintain their shape, although they are quite fragile.

Cuisines and Crafts

The berries make wonderful jellies and pies, while the blooms add a tart, floralish flavor to fritters and crepes. The lacy flowers also make a nice tea. The berries can be frozen in the summer and used throughout the winter as filler fruit for pies and desserts.

Although they're fragile, the blooms look lovely in wreaths, garlands, and on hat bands. The berries look nice in crafts such as arrangements and wreaths, and are especially nice in projects that use lots of moss. The dried blooms can be stored in an opaque container and displayed where they'll be enjoyed.

Fennel

Fennel's distinctive fragrance and flavor has earned it several nicknames, including licorice plant, sweet fennel, and finocchio. This close relative to dill grows 4 to 6 feet (1.2 to 1.8 m) tall, making it a stunning choice for the back of an herb garden. It grows well in full sun and well-drained soil, and attracts both bees and butterflies. Fennel should be given lots of room when you first put it in your garden so it has room to spread.

Drying

Since fennel seeds are well loved, many herb gardeners prefer to dry the blooms by placing a small paper bag over a small bundle and then hanging the bouquet upside down to dry. The blooms develop a goldish color as they dry and are fairly sturdy. Harvest them at their peak if you plan to use them in craft projects; harvest them after their peak if you plan to cook with them so the seeds will have a chance to ripen.

The gossamer-like quality of fennel's foliage makes it worth drying, even though it shrinks quite a bit and is not very sturdy. The foliage can be harvested at any time, and dries best when laid flat on a screen rack, hung upside down in small bundles, or microwaved without silica gel for a short time. Both the blooms and foliage also dry well by pressing.

Cuisines and Crafts

Fennel leaves can be crumbled and sprinkled over salads or kept whole and wrapped around fish before cooking. The seeds add a zesty flavor to salads, applesauce, and apple pies, and can also be simmered in boiling water with a few leaves for a tea that reputedly decreases the appetite and relieves gas. The bulbs of Foeniculum vulgare are known as a great delicacy. Dig them up in the fall, brush with them olive oil, and roast in foil. Eat the roasted bulbs as is, or slice them thinly and add them to salads, stews, and soups.

Fennel flowers and foliage add a fairy-like appeal to bouquets, wreaths, hats, garlands, and many other craft projects.

Monarda, Chives & Sage

Carnations, Bay
& Lavender

Feverfew

Feverfew is a gardener's dream incarnate: it blooms and self-sows prolifically with little care. This perennial will come back in full force every year, so be sure to allow it lots of room. The white flowers with yellow centers resemble miniature daisies, and the foliage is a golden green. Feverfew thrives in full to partial sun and in soil with good drainage. Some people find the plant's light fragrance pleasing, although an almost equal number do not.

Drying

Feverfew blooms shrink very little as they dry and retain their color well. The leaves curl a little and also retain their color. The blooms can be harvested for drying at any time during the growth cycle, while the leaves should be harvested before the plant blooms. Stems of feverfew can be grouped together and hung upside down to dry. The blooms and foliage can be separated and arranged on a screen rack or dried by pressing. The blooms also dry well in the microwave when arranged on a paper towel and cooked for one to one-and-a-half minutes. The blooms also press well.

Cuisines and Crafts

In Europe, feverfew leaves are infused in teas and eaten with eggs and sandwiches. Many people still hold value in the herbal lore that advocates chewing a few leaves to relieve headaches and migraines, and most major medical associations acknowledge feverfew's abilities. (Note: Before you try to relieve your next headache this way, be sure to sample one leaf first and watch for allergic reactions.)

Feverfew flowers add a delicate touch to almost any craft, the most popular being wreaths, potpourris, and arrangements.

Garlic

Garlic has been attributed all sorts of interesting powers through the centuries, including the ability to repel vampires and, according to Culpepper's 1649 *Color Herbal*, help with "the biting of mad dogs, and other venomous creatures." In Culpepper's time, garlic was considered the ideal herbal drug for the less prosperous segments of society because it reportedly had some healing effects on virtually every ill. (The more prosperous segments of society were able to purchase a different herb for each ailment.) Garlic thrives in rich, well-drained soil in full sun with frequent waterings. Once the plants get started, they spread easily.

Drying

Harvest the flowers in the spring before they begin to fade. Harvest the bulbs in late summer and handle them gently until they dry. The seed heads and flowers can be dried separately on screen racks or left attached to stems of foliage and hung upside down in small bundles. The seed heads form a striking design when pressed. The dried blooms are attractive but very delicate. The foliage darkens slightly and loses some of its tangy fragrance.

Cuisines and Crafts

Garlic's prevalence in recipes makes it an invaluable resource for most cooks. Whole bulbs can be roasted in the oven for a surprisingly sweet and memorable appetizer. Just brush them with olive oil, cover with aluminum foil, and bake at 350° F (180° C) for an hour.

Garlic seed heads and blooms look nice in bouquets, wreaths, garlands, and swags. The bulbs can be hot-glued into wreaths, garlands, and swags, or woven into a garlic braid that can then be decorated with chili peppers, bay leaves, and/or colorful blooms.

Carnations, Bay & Lavender

Roses, Lamb's Ears, & Scented Geraniums

Germander

A perennial shrub with dark green foliage, germander averages 18 to 24 inches (46 to 61 cm) and makes an attractive border plant in knot gardens. Since germander tends to get a little shaggy, though, it needs frequent pruning. The only negative to using germander as a border plant is that you will miss out on the charming purple/rose flowers because of the prunings.

Drying

Germander leaves can be harvested at any time; experiment with harvesting the blooms at different times in the growth cycle. Hang and screen drying as well as pressing work well for both the foliage and the blooms. The flowers retain their color very well when dried in silica gel, but they shrink a lot and become extremely fragile. The leaves will dry acceptably in a microwave but the blooms will not. The leaves remain sturdy after drying and shrink very little, while the blooms become fragile and tend to shrink a lot.

Crafts

The colorful dried blooms can be hot-glued individually into wreath and garland bases, or arranged on top of potpourris as a decorative accent. Stems of foliage and blooms can be arranged in bouquets or attached to floral picks and used in arrangements and wreaths.

Heather

This carefree herb is very popular in Europe, Asia Minor, and Scotland. It likes full to partial sun and a semi-acid soil. The blooms are a light pink and resemble miniature lanterns in shape. White heather, when found in the wild, is reputedly a symbol of good luck.

Drying

Harvest your heather at its peak to ensure as many blooms as possible. Screen drying and pressing work well for the blooms. Hang drying also works well, but only if you plan to keep the bunches together after they're dry. (The leaves and blooms will fall off if you try to separate them.) After drying, the light green leaves begin fading to a golden yellow; the blooms retain their charming shape and pink color. Both the leaves and the foliage are very fragile and shatter when touched.

Crafts

Single heather blooms make colorful touches to potpourris. For wreath making, stems of fresh-cut heather can be worked around a wire base and secured loosely with monofilament. The wreaths should then be hung in a moisture-free location where they can dry undisturbed. Since the finished wreaths will be so delicate, choose a hanging location where they won't be bumped or brushed against.

Roses, Lamb's Ears, & Scented Geraniums

Monarda, Chives & Sage

Horehound

Horehound grows up to 3 feet (91 cm) tall in warmer climates and thrives in full sun. This perennial spreads quickly, and the only special care it needs is protection from heavy winds.

Drying

The whitish-gray foliage is soft and fuzzy when fresh and similar when dry. Harvest your horehound while it's in bloom and hang it upside down to dry in small bunches. The foliage dries with lovely curves, shrinks very little, and is remarkably sturdy. The blooms do not dry well with the hanging method, although they look nice when pressed. If you're in a rush, the microwave can be used for drying as long as you don't plan to use the horehound for culinary purposes.

Cuisines and Crafts

Horehound is still used today as a cough remedy, and the following recipe is an easy way to make homemade cough drops. Boil 1/4 cup of dried horehound leaves with 2 cups of water for 10 minutes. Allow the mixture to cool for 20 minutes. Strain out the leaves and mix 1 cup of the infusion with 2 cups of sugar and a dash of cream of tartar. Stir well until the sugar dissolves and then cook the mixture over a very low heat until a drop forms a hard, glassy ball when dropped into cold water. Pour the mixture onto a well-buttered marble slab or plate. Quickly score into small squares. Store the cough drops in the refrigerator.

Horehound's variegated foliage and striking flower spikes make wonderful additions to wreaths, garlands, and arrangements. The flower spikes can also be used in potpourris.

Lamb's Ear

This fascinating perennial is a favorite of bees, children, and curious adults. The fuzzy leaves actually do resemble lamb's ears, and they were once used as primitive bandages. The plant needs virtually no care; just place it in full sun and pinch off the leaves as they brown. With its gray foliage and tall, purple flower spikes, lamb's ear makes a lovely border plant in gardens. It spreads like wild, though, so you may need to thin it occasionally to contain it and keep the roots from molding.

Drying

Lamb's ear leaves can be harvested in different growth stages for a variety of interesting sizes. Spread the leaves out on a screen rack and turn every few days. The leaves curl slightly as they dry, but not enough to distract from their beauty. The small, pink-to-purple blooms on the flower spikes tend to shrivel up and lose some of their color, but the spikes themselves have an interesting shape and are worth drying.

To dry the flower spikes, harvest them when they first begin to bloom and then hang them upside down in small bunches. Screen drying works well for the individual leaves. Stems of foliage and blooms can also be preserved with glycerin by soaking the stems in a glycerin/water mixture for three days. Glycerin-preserved stems and leaves are more pliable for arrangements and maintain their shape and texture beautifully.

Crafts

The alluring tactile qualities of lamb's ear makes it a wonderful choice for wreaths, arrangements, and potpourris. Single leaves can be hot-glued into a background material, while stems can be cut at an angle and inserted directly into a moss, straw, or foam base.

Monarda, Chives & Sage

Carnations, Bay & Lavender

Lavender

Few herbs can compete with lavender's popularity over the centuries. Culpepper's Herbal, originally published in 1649, recommends lavender baths to relieve colic symptoms and distilled lavender water to "reduce the tremblings and passions of the heart, and faintings and swoonings . . ." Today, lavender oil is the fragrance base for many soaps, air fresheners, and perfumes.

Lavender prefers a sunny, open place to grow, and many of the varieties grow by leaps and bounds in just one season. Bees love lavender, and the only care the plants require is a little cutting back in autumn. There are numerous varieties of lavender to choose from: Hidcote and munstead are the favorites of many professional herb gardeners, although English, French, Spanish, spike, and wooily also make nice choices.

Drying

Lavender spikes should be harvested at the peak of their bloom. They can be air-dried on screens or by hanging, and also press well. (The French and Spanish varieties tend to be too fleshy to press well.) Since lavender's primary attraction is its fragrance, microwave drying should be avoided. Lavender varieties with purple and deep blue blooms retain their colors well after drying, while the pinkish blooms tend to fade as they dry.

Lavender

Cuisines and Crafts

We're so used to enjoying lavender's fragrance, that many people never think to enjoy lavender's flavor. Lavender honey can be made by pouring warm honey over two lavender spikes, covering the container, and allowing the flavor to infuse for two weeks. Lavender syrups, marmalades, and vinegars are also great ways to enjoy the flavor of this versatile herb. And if you like making homemade ice creams, lavender ice cream will soon become your favorite.

Dried lavender is a crafter's dream material: It's gorgeous to look at, relatively sturdy, and the fragrance is always a pleasure. Lavender is a frequent choice for potpourris — either as the primary ingredient or as a fragrance accent. Lavender-based potpourris are also popular in small dream pillows and sachets.

Wreaths are another popular way to showcase dried lavender. Make a lavender wreath by attaching 4-inch (10 cm) lengths one at a time to a wire ring base with thin-gauge floral wire or monofilament. You can display the wreath as is, or hot-glue miniature rosebuds or other delicate materials into the lavender.

Carnations, Bay & Lavender

Roses, Lamb's Ears, & Scented Geraniums

Lemon Balm

Named after and loved for its lemon fragrance, this 1- to 3-foot (30 to 91 cm) perennial likes full sun to partial shade and appreciates a top dressing of mulch or worm castings in the fall and spring. Lemon balm is a favorite of bees and requires virtually no care. Plant this herb in an area of your garden or yard where you'd like to see lots more lemon balm because it self sows prolifically and spreads in large clumps.

Drying

For culinary use, harvest the leaves before the plant blooms; for use in potpourris and other crafts, you can harvest at any time during the growth cycle. The small white blooms do not dry well, but the shape of the flower stalk dries true to form if harvested when they first begin to bloom.

The leaves can be hung upside down in small bunches or spread out individually on a screen. The leaves can also be microwaved without silica gel or pressed. (Note: If you decide to press lemon balm, be sure to save the pressing paper since it will absorb the lemony fragrance.)

The pale, greenish-yellow foliage lightens slightly and curls up on the edges as it dries. It shrinks down to about 60% of its original size, and retains much of its lemony fragrance. The dried foliage is very fragile — almost like tissue paper — and crumbles easily, so be very careful if you plan to use them in a craft project.

Cuisines and Crafts

Lemon balm leaves can be steeped in boiling water for a few minutes for a delightful herbal tea. Dried, crumbled leaves can also be used to flavor fruit salads, mayonnaise, mixed drinks, vinegars, cake frostings, and worked into bread doughs before cooking.

Lemon balm's most popular craft use is in potpourris. They can be displayed in your favorite bowl or used to fill small muslin bags to tie around the water spout in the tub for a soothing bath. Fresh-cut lemon balm can also be used to make wreaths by gently weaving the stems of foliage and blooms around a wire ring base and securing in place with loose wraps of monofilament. After the wreath has dried, your favorite colorful blooms, such as calendula and bee balm, can then be hot-glued into the lemon balm.

Lemon Verbena

Appropriately named for its lemony fragrance and taste, this tender perennial averages 1 to 2 feet (30 to 61 cm) in most zones and grows up to 8 to 9 feet (2.4 to 2.7 m) in very warm regions. Lemon verbena needs little care, although it can die very quickly when planted in areas with poor soil drainage. The foliage is primarily green with tinges of yellow, and the tiny blooms are white and pale purple.

Drying

The leaves can be harvested at any time during the growth cycle, while the blooms should be harvested when they first begin to open. The leaves and blooms dry best when arranged in small bunches and hung upside down. They can also be pressed or dried individually on a screen rack. The leaves curl a bit as they dry, although their pungent fragrance remains for years.

Cuisines and Crafts

Lemon verbena leaves can impart their rich citrus flavor in numerous recipes, including teas, jellies, vinegars, cookies, breads, and ice creams.

In crafts, the leaves can be used individually in potpourris, sachets, sleep pillows, and as a facial steam. Fragrant lemon verbena wreaths can also be made by bending fresh-cut stems into a circle or heart shape, securing them in place with a little floral wire, and allowing them to dry in a dark, moisture-free environment. The wreaths can then be embellished with small herb blooms such as roses or lavender if desired.

Roses, Lamb's Ears, & Scented Geraniums

Monarda, Chives & Sage

Lovage

Native to the mountainous regions of the Mediterranean, this herb ranges between 4 and 7 feet (1.2 to 2 m) in height, and likes to be planted in fertile, well-drained soil. Lovage needs little care, spreads easily, and attracts lots of butterflies, although it can be temperamental if not watered frequently. Lovage's glossy foliage and delicate yellow flowers makes this a nice herb to border the back of a garden.

Drying

The leaves can be harvested at any time during the growth cycle, although be careful not to pick too many of the young, central leaves to avoid damaging the plant. Harvest the flowers at the peak of their bloom for crafts, or after they've finished blooming if you're after the seeds.

Hang stems of the blooms and leaves upside down to dry or arrange them loosely on a screen rack. Lovage can be dried with a microwave but it overdries very quickly, so begin with a short length of time and add extra time in small amounts, if needed. The blooms also press well. The leaves are rather fragile and often curled around their edges, although they do retain much of their celery-like fragrance. The blooms retain their shape and color well.

Cuisines and Crafts

Lovage leaves add a wonderful taste to soups, salads, cheeses, and salt-free blends, while the seeds work well sprinkled in cordials and over mashed potatoes. Children get a big thrill using straws made from hollow lovage stems. To make the straws, harvest the stems at any time the plant is blooming and choose the widest ones.

Marjoram

This 12- to 18-inch (30 to 46 cm) perennial likes full sun and well-drained soil. It spreads beautifully and needs little care except for an occasional knot trim. Marjoram has a sweet, oregano-like taste and fragrance that makes it a good strewing herb. Since marjoram historically signifies joy, it can be used to make symbolic gifts to celebrate special occasions such as weddings and births.

Drying

Marjoram should be harvested at the peak of its bloom so you'll get the lovely "knots." Marjoram dries well on screens, hanging upside down, or with pressing. It will also dry in the microwave, but it browns easily so begin with a short time and add short amounts of additional time if needed. The foliage retains its light green color, shrinks very little, and is quite sturdy. A light fragrance is present in the dried foliage.

Cuisines and Crafts

Marjoram's flavors blend well with other herbs, making it a good herb to include in bouquet garnis and salt-free seasoning mixes. To make a bouquet garni, mix the dried marjoram with parsley, thyme, tarragon, and bay. Fill small cheesecloth or tea bags with the herbs and add them to sauces, stews, and soups as they cook. A good seasoning mix recipe is to mix dried marjoram with oregano, rosemary, thyme, savory, and a few lavender budlets.

Marjoram makes a good base material for wreaths, hats, swags, and garlands. Culinary accents, such as garlic bulbs, cinnamon sticks, and star anise, can then be hot-glued into marjoram base. Marjoram's symbolic past also makes it a good material to include in bridal bouquets.

Monarda, Chives & Sage

Carnations, Bay & Lavender

Mint

Several mints, such as peppermint and spearmint, have become so entrenched in day-to-day living that many people never associate the zesty flavors in their favorite toothpastes and chewing gums with these free-spirited herbs. Mints come in lots of other flavors too, such as orange, lemon, grapefruit, lime, ginger, chocolate, apple, and spice.

Mint needs little care if you don't mind it taking over your garden; otherwise, you'll need to separate it frequently for transplanting or sharing with friends. To do this, just cut through the mint in a waffle pattern and the mint will fill in the spaces. Most mints adapt well to wherever they're planted — full sun or shade. Just be careful not to plant different varieties too close or they'll cross-pollinate. (If your garden space is limited, you can plant them in buckets and pinch off the blooms to prevent the flavors from mixing.)

Drying

Harvest the leaves before the plant blooms if you plan to use it in a culinary project; for craft projects, the leaves and blooms can be harvested at any time during the growth cycle. Mint dries well by hanging, screen drying, and pressing. Expect the leaves to curl, shrink, and become fairly fragile as they dry, although much of the characteristic fragrance remains.

Cuisines and Crafts

Mint teas are simple to make — just steep a few leaves in boiling water until the tea reaches a satisfactory strength. The leaves also add a decorative touch to mixed drinks and a nice flavor to salt-free spice blends.

Mint leaves and blooms look and smell wonderful in wreaths, small bouquets, potpourris, and bath blends. Since the leaves can be so delicate when dry, you may have more success arranging them in wreaths and bouquets when they're fresh-cut and then allowing them to dry in place.

Mugwort

Mugwort's intriguing common names — traveler's herb and ale herb — hint at this plant's involvement in herbal folklore over the centuries. In the days when the primary method of transportation was walking, placing a leaf of mugwort in your shoes reputedly enabled travelers to walk 40 miles without fatigue, and the leaves were also used to flavor mugs of ale. This perennial herb averages 2 to 5 feet (.6 to 1.5 m), has lovely, silver/green leaves, and has a wonderful fragrance that has been described as a cross between mint and resin. The plant grows easily and spreads well — even in poor soils and disturbed areas — and tends to be pest free.

Drying

Mugwort leaves and blooms can be harvested at any time during the growth cycle. They dry fast and beautifully when hung upside down in small bundles or when pressed. (Screen drying also works, but it's not worth your time to spread them out when hang drying works so well.) The leaves darken, curl, and become brittle as they dry, although most of the fragrance remains. The blooms shrink a little but are fairly sturdy.

Crafts

Mugwort makes a nice addition to herbal wreaths, bringing an airy look and a refreshing fragrance. Wreath bases can be made from mugwort by arranging the fresh-cut stems inside a basket and then securing them in a circle shape with monofilament after they've dried. Both the flowers and the leaves reputedly repel moths, and are often used to fill sachets for clothing closets. The fragrant leaves are an ingredient in traditional dream pillows.

Carnations, Bay & Lavender

Roses, Lamb's Ears,
& Scented Geraniums

Parsley

Although most people tend to think of parsley as a culinary herb, it was used in the 1600s exclusively for medicinal treatments. This biennial herb likes rich, moist soil, and isn't picky about how much (or how little) sun it gets. Once established, parsley needs little care.

Drying

The foliage shrinks about 50% and turns to a golden olive green during the drying process. There is usually some curling of the leaves, although not enough to make it unattractive. If you're planning to use the parsley for culinary projects, the leaves should be harvested when they're still young and tender and before the plant blooms. (Many culinary enthusiasts believe that the taste becomes too bitter after the plant is a year old and plant a new parsley crop every year.) For craft use, do your harvesting after the light yellow blooms appear. Because dried parsley is so delicate, it's best to dry it on a rack or in the microwave.

Cuisines and Crafts

Parsley makes a wonderful herbal complement to egg and potato dishes, as well as soups, salads, and fish. It's usually best to add the parsley at the end of the cooking time. The roots can also be harvested, boiled, and then grated over salads.

Because dried parsley is so delicate, it is not a good background material to form wreaths or arrangements. It can be arranged in small bouquets, though, and used as an accent material in wreaths and garlands. Fresh-cut parsley arranged with bright-colored roses makes a lovely centerpiece for special occasions, and the parsley can then be dried afterwards to flavor next season's soups.

Pennyroyal

This member of the mint family has been attributed all sorts of medicinal powers over the centuries. Its ancient reputation for stimulating the menstrual cycle had many people believing pennyroyal could induce a miscarriage, although modern medicine disputes this idea.

This perennial likes a moist, shady place to grow, and left undiscouraged, will spread into a wonderful thick mat. The blooms grow out from the mat in stalks about 18 inches (46 cm) high.

Drying

Pennyroyal dries well by hanging upside down in small bundles. The leaves and flowers also dry well on a screen, although you'll need to turn them frequently to prevent mold from forming. The leaves curl slightly as they dry, but they're well worth drying since they retain so much of their minty fragrance and the dark green foliage is lovely. The stems and flowers retain much of their mauve to blue to purple coloring and hold their shape well. The leaves and blooms dry well with pressing or by standing them upright to air dry.

Cuisines and Crafts

Since it's a member of the mint family, it shouldn't surprise you that pennyroyal makes a fragrant, minty tea. It can also be used to flavor soups and sauces, but should be used sparingly because it's so pungent.

Pennyroyal reputedly repels moths and fleas, so it's often made into a potpourri and then used to fill sachets that can then be tied around coat hangers of wool clothing, folded in with sweaters, or even tied around a pet's neck as a natural flea collar. One popular potpourri recipe includes equal amounts of pennyroyal, tansy, silver king artemisia, cedar bark curls, cloves, and southernwood.

Pennyroyal also makes a good pet shampoo and human insect repellent: just puree the leaves and stems in a blender. A wonderful gardener's hat that repels insects can be made by hot-gluing fresh-cut pennyroyal, coneflowers, and yarrow around a straw hat's rim and then allowing the materials to air-dry in place.

Roses, Lamb's Ears, & Scented Geraniums

Monarda, Chives
& Sage

Queen Anne's Lace

Also known as bird's nest, this 1- to 4-foot (.3 to 1.2 m) biennial is actually a type of wild carrot and was once a staple in several earlier cultures' diets. Although you may want to cultivate Queen Anne's lace in a sunny, dry location in your garden, it grows so prolifically in some areas in open fields and on roadsides that you may not want to take up garden space with it.

Drying

Harvest the leaves at any time; harvest the blooms at any time during the growth cycle before they go to seed. Harvest the roots after the plant has bloomed but before they become old and tough. (Be sure to use caution when harvesting the roots: The roadside plants are often sprayed with herbicides and the roots resemble those of hemlock.)

The blooms dry well with a variety of methods: hanging, screen rack drying (push each stem down through a separate hole so the bloom rests flat), upright air drying, pressing, and with desiccants. Blooms picked very early and very late in the blooming cycle will curl a lot as they dry, but they're very attractive when mixed with the larger, flat blooms. You can achieve a variety of colors by placing several fresh-cut bloom stems in a vase filled with water and a few drops of food coloring, and then drying the plant as usual.

Cuisines and Crafts

The roots can be boiled and eaten as a vegetable, and the flower seeds can be used to add a light carrot flavor to salads and breads.

The delicate blooms resemble lace doilies, and look wonderful in wreaths, arrangements, potpourris, and pressed pictures.

Rose

In the 1600s, this ancient herb was revered for reputed medicinal powers, while in Victorian times it was popular for its symbolic meanings of love, pride, and grace. Today, roses are grown for their floral beauty and alluring fragrances. Hybridization has given us varieties with blooms in almost every color, from antique white to dark maroon, and the fragrances vary from spicy to the traditional floral "rose" scent.

Drying

If you plan to air-dry your roses, they should be harvested when they're still in a tight bud or slightly opened. If you plan to use a desiccant to dry them, they can be harvested at any stage of the blooming cycle. A mixture of half borax and half cornmeal works well with roses in full bloom. If you're drying roses for potpourri, the individual petals can be spread out on a drying screen and turned every few days. Individual petals can also be pressed, and the pressing paper will have a lovely rose fragrance.

During air-drying, some rose varieties will darken in color; color and shape retention is best when they're dried in silica gel. With desiccant drying you can also dry blooms that have fully opened up with some success.

Cuisines and Crafts

Rose-flavored condiments, such as jellies, syrups, vinegars, and butters, are an Old World delicacy to be savored. Rose petals can also be sprinkled on ice creams, sorbets, and cakes with tasteful and decorative results. In Sweden, soup made from rose hips is a favorite, and it's high in vitamins A and C. Caution: All roses used in culinary projects should be free from insecticides.

For crafts, roses add a classic look to everything from arrangements to topiaries to wreaths. Dried rose buds can be porcelained with one of the mixtures available in craft stores and then made into jewelry, and rose petals are a long-time favorite of potpourri makers. Rose hips are a big bonus to crafters, adding nice touches to potpourris and autumn wreaths.

Monarda, Chives & Sage

Carnations, Bay & Lavender

Rosemary

Also known as dew-of-the-sea, rosemary can be cultivated as a small potted plant or in the garden up to 5 feet (1.5 m) in height. This tender perennial needs to be brought indoors during cold winters, and likes full sun and a nice mulching every now and then.

Drying

Long stems of rosemary can be hung upside down to dry, while smaller sprigs can be arranged on a screen rack. The needles curl slightly as they dry and have a tendency to fall off when handled. There is little shrinkage and the piney fragrance remains strong. If you have lots of rosemary and would like to make a wreath, it's better to arrange the fresh-cut rosemary in a circle shape and then hang it to dry. The plant's essential oil is so strong that you can dry it in the microwave without silica gel for about a minute without losing much flavor. Rosemary also presses beautifully.

Cuisines and Crafts

For serious cooks, rosemary is indispensable. While it's probably best known for its effect on lamb, rosemary also makes a flavorful impact in sauces, pastas, and vinegars. A versatile way to preserve your rosemary is to spend the next rainy day making rosemary butters and pestos for the freezer. If you can find some nice small jars, these culinary treats make wonderful gifts.

Rosemary topiaries are a challenge but worth the effort; you can start them yourself with the help of a good book or you can purchase one that's been started for you at an herb farm. Sprigs of dried rosemary make a nice embellishment for garlic braids, garden hats, garlands, and culinary wreaths, and are also a pleasant ingredient in potpourris.

Rue

Also known as the herb of grace, this small perennial shrub was once revered for its ability to repel witches and evil spirits when planted at the front door. And even today, gardeners who enjoy reading old herbal folklores will often plant some rue by their front door for good luck. Rue likes partial sun and dry soil, and does not spread much. Rue oil is commonly used in the manufacturing of manufacture toiletries and cosmetics, and a homemade insect repellant for your plants can be made by pouring boiling water over a mixture of rue, tansy, and wormwood.

Drying

Harvest the leaves at any time during the growth cycle and the bright yellow flowers when they first begin to bloom. Dry by hanging upside down in small bunches or pressing. The leaves curl as they dry and lose much of their musky fragrance, while the blooms will shrink some and darken as they dry. Since rue can induce allergic reactions in some people, you may wish to handle this herb with extra care.

Crafts

Rue's delicate yellow flowers look lovely scattered on top of a large bowl of potpourri. The flowers can also be worked into wreaths and arrangements when fresh and left to dry in place. Since rue can cause allergic reactions in many people, you may wish to handle the herbs with gloves.

Carnations, Bay & Lavender

Roses, Lamb's Ears,
& Scented Geraniums

Safflower

This cheerful annual is known for its bright, golden orange blooms and olive-colored foliage. Many herbalists believe the seeds will lower cholesterol, while the flowers are used by native Americans as a natural dye.

Drying

Both blooms and foliage dry well: the blooms retain their brilliant color and are quite sturdy, while the leaves develop an attractive curl on their edges. Harvest stems of safflowers when the blooms have peaked and hang them upside down in small bunches to dry. If you don't have need of the foliage, the blooms can be dried individually on a screen rack. Desiccants also work well, but the effort isn't warranted when the blooms dry so well with easier methods.

Cuisines and Crafts

Some people use safflower petals as a substitute for saffron, although many other cooks say the only thing the two herbs have in common is color and a similar name.

Safflower blooms are ideal for swags, garlands, wreaths, arrangements, and potpourris. The bright orange color makes them especially attractive in autumn crafts.

Sage

Once cultivated for medicinal use (it was mixed with rosemary, honeysuckle, and plantain for a gargle), sage is now grown for its culinary and aesthetic qualities. Sage comes in several hundred varieties: some perennials, some annuals; some tall, some short; some culinary, some purely decorative; some variegated, some not. Most sages like full sun and a well-drained soil. They spread easily and attract lots of butterflies, bees, and hummingbirds.

Common garden sage (*Salvia officinalis*) is probably the most well known of all the sages. It's a hardy perennial shrub that averages 3 feet (91 cm) in height. It's leaves are a grayish green and are saturated with the pungent oil we all recognize as the smell of sage. Two other popular varieties of Salvia officinalis include the golden sage (*Salvia officinalis aurea*), which features variegated yellow and gray leaves, and purple sage (*Salvia officinalis 'Purpurea*), which comes in several shades of purple.

Clary sage (*Salvia sclarea*) is difficult to cultivate but very beautiful. Its large leaves grow close to the ground and the plant's lilac blooms are comparatively long-lasting. Clary sage is a biennial that averages 2 to 3 feet (61 to 91 cm) in height. Mexican sage makes an attractive hedge plant and attracts lots of hummingbirds. Another variety, Clevelandii, is used to fix fragrances in potpourris.

Pineapple sage (*Salvia elegans*) has dark green foliage and brilliant scarlet blooms. It's an annual in some locations and a tender perennial in others, and averages 3 to 5 feet (.3 to 1.5 m) in height. If this variety of sage is new to you, you'll be amazed at how closely its fragrances resembles pineapple fruit. Another variety of sage known as variegated sage (*Salvia officinalis tricolor*), dazzles gardeners with its beautiful pink, rose, and green colored foliage. This variety is a perennial that averages 1 to 2 feet (30 to 61 cm) in height.

(continues on page 84)

Roses, Lamb's Ears, & Scented Geraniums

Monarda, Chives & Sage

Sage

(continued on page 83)

Drying

Sage foliage can be harvested at any time, while the blooms should be harvested at their peak. You'll get good results drying most of the sages described above using hanging, screen drying, and pressing. The edible sages also dry well in the microwave without silica gel. Clevelandii and some of the other sages dry well with upright air-drying, although Mexican and elegans will droop with this method. The colors tend to fade a little, and about 75% of the fragrances are retained. (Clevelandii is a fragrance exception — it retains 100% of its wonderful fragrance.)

Cuisines and Crafts

If you like the flavor of sage, it soon becomes a mainstay in your cooking. Turkey, chicken, stuffings, salads, dressings, stews, and many other items all benefit from sage's flavoring. Pineapple sage imparts its fruity flavor in lots of recipes (chicken and carrots are favorites of many cooks), and since you can use both the leaves and the blooms, it adds lots of color. You can make a wonderful tea with common garden sage by steeping the leaves and several quartered lemons in boiling water and then serving the tea steaming hot or iced.

Sage blooms and foliage make wonderful additions as accents to wreaths, garlands, hats, and small bouquets. Sage also makes a nice background material in wreaths and garlands, and almost any variety of herb bloom looks nice nestled into it. Because dried sage can be a little brittle, you may want to arrange it in your crafts while it's fresh and let it dry in place.

Salad Burnet

A 2-foot (61 cm) perennial, salad burnet spreads easily and needs no special care, making it a nice choice for garden borders. The fresh green foliage is lovely, and the blooms are interesting to watch as they develop small green blooms intermixed with even smaller rose-pink blooms.

Drying

Unfortunately, the small pink blooms drop off during drying; the green blooms retain their color but are very fragile. Some people like to dry only the young, tender leaves, although the plant can be harvested at any stage. The plant can be air-dried by hanging, and your bundles should only have two or three stems in them. The leaves dry well on screen racks if turned frequently, and both the leaves and blooms dry well by pressing.

Cuisines and Crafts

Salad burnet's leaves have a nutty, cucumber-like flavor that can be used to flavor cheese blends, vinegars, teas, cream soups, casseroles, and salads. The herb also works well in just about any recipe calling for rosemary and/or tarragon. Fresh-picked leaves can also be sprinkled over salads.

The dried knotheads add a nice touch to potpourris, and the feathery leaves look nice in wreaths, although you should add them last to prevent breakage. The pressed leaves are a little stronger, and can be used to embellish the sides of candles or to create pressed pictures and note cards.

Monarda, Chives & Sage

Carnations, Bay & Lavender

Santolina

Despite the implications of its common name, lavender cotton, santolina is actually a member of the daisy family. In the mid-1600s, Culpepper reported in his *Color Herbal* that santolina was "boiled in milk and taken fasting" to destroy worms. The plant averages about 2 feet (61 cm) in height, and does best when planted in full sun and well-drained soil. The foliage is usually a shimmering gray color, and their shapes resemble those of fine laces. Santolina fills out quickly and loves to be clipped into hedges. If you decide not to clip it back, it will tend to get a little woody and floppy but will reward you with golden yellow button blooms. Although santolina is a perennial in most areas, it will need to be protected with a thick layer of mulch if your winter temperatures dip much below freezing.

Drying

The leaves can be gathered for drying at any time during the growth cycle. They maintain much of their size, shape, and color as they dry, and even keep a hint of their fruity fragrance. Single leaves can be dried flat on a screen rack, while stems of leaves do best if arranged in small bouquets and hung upside down. The flowers do best if dropped by their stems through a screen rack or microwaved for a short length of time. Both the foliage and the blooms press well.

Crafts

Santolina's strong stems make it an ideal herb for wreaths and arrangements. Instead of having to create faux stems with wire or floral picks, just cut the end of the stem at an angle to make perforation into a base easier. The leaves are also a common ingredient in recipes for moth and flea repellant potpourris. Santolina's button flowers add a burst of sunshine to garlands, swags, wreaths, decorated hats, potpourris, and many other craft projects.

Scented Geranium

This plant has amazed gardeners for centuries with its ability to adopt the fragrances of nearby plants. You'll find scented geraniums with rose, peppermint, cinnamon, coconut, almond, apricot, apple, and nutmeg scents, just to name the most popular. Scented geraniums tend to thrive in shaded areas in light, humus soil. Gardeners who live in areas with very warm winters may find that this herb spreads like a weed. In colder climates, this tender perennial will need to be potted and brought indoors for the winter.

Drying

Most scented geranium leaves lose their beautiful green colors and turn brown as they dry, but they do keep most of their fragrance, making them a wonderful choice for potpourri recipes. The leaves curl as they dry and lose their strong fragrance, although the fragrance can be rejuvenated by crumbling a few leaves between your fingers. To dry, just arrange the leaves on a screen and turn every few days. If you don't want the leaves to curl, you can press them with excellent results. The drying results of scented geranium blooms vary with the variety: the pink and pink/red blooms retain their color, while the white blooms shrivel up and turn brown.

Cuisines and Crafts

Scented geranium leaves can be added to sugar cookies and homemade breads with wonderful results. Flavored sugars can also be made by filling a small jar with sugar and several whole, fresh leaves and allowing the geranium flavors to saturate the sugar for three to four weeks. The leaves and flowers from cinnamon and nutmeg geraniums taste wonderful in fruit salads, while many of the other varieties add a splash of flavor to dinner salads.

All varieties of scented geraniums work well in potpourris. Pressed geranium leaves have beautiful shapes that can be showcased on note cards, picture frames, and candles, just to name a few places.

Carnations, Bay & Lavender

Roses, Lamb's Ears, & Scented Geraniums

Silver King & Queen Artemisias

These silvery members of the artemisia family are easy to grow and make attractive members of any herb garden. Averaging about 3 feet (91 cm) in height, the taller 'Silver King' artemisia makes a nice hedge plant, while the shorter 'Silver Queen' artemisia, averaging about 1-1/2 feet (46 cm) makes a nice border plant. Both varieties like to be planted in full sun in well-drained soil. Be sure to keep the plants thinned out as they spread, especially if you've had a very wet season, to prevent the roots from rotting.

Drying

Both varieties can be harvested at any time during the growth cycle, although crafters who like the small, berry-like blooms on 'Silver King' artemisia should wait until late in the summer to harvest. Both plants can be hung upside down in small bunches or pressed, with very little loss in size, shape, or color. Because the 'Silver King' variety is so rigid once it's dry, you may wish to add curves by coiling fresh-cut stems around the inside of a basket or other round object.

Crafts

Both varieties are valued in potpourris for their attractive silver color and their reputed ability to repel moths. Artemisia is also the perfect choice for wreaths, bouquets, garlands, and swags, either as a background material or to add colorful accents. Artemisia wreaths can be made by arranging fresh-cut stems around a wreath base and securing them in place with monofilament. Place the wreath in a dark, moisture-free location and remove it after all of the foliage has dried.

Anise

Native to the Middle East and sometimes known as sweet anise, the light yellow/white blooms on this 2- to 3-foot (30 to 61 cm) annual attract lots of butterflies. It needs little care, and likes full sun and a loose, fast-draining soil.

Drying

For the seeds and the blooms, harvest the flower stalks when they're at the peak of their bloom; the foliage can be harvested at any time. Dry the blooms and foliage by hanging, pressing, or arranging on a screen rack. The smaller pressed blooms tend to be especially attractive. To collect the seeds, place a small paper bag over the flower stalk, secure with a rubber band, and hang dry as usual. The flower stalks dry well as long as they're not harvested when they contain lots of moisture; the foliage curls a bit but retains a light licorice-like aroma.

Cuisines and Crafts

Sweet anise adds pizazz to a vast variety of foods. The leaves can be added to egg dishes, salads and dressings, and cream cheeses. The seeds can be mixed into sauces, dressings, and lots of desserts and baked goods. Since the flavor is most concentrated in the seeds, you'll get the best results by fresh-grinding the seeds just before use.

The flower stalks look lovely in potpourris, wreaths, garlands and dried arrangements.

Roses, Lamb's Ears, & Scented Geraniums

Monarda, Chives & Sage

Sweet Annie

Commonly known as Chinese Christmas fern, sweet wormwood, and botanically as Artemisia annua, this tall (up to 6 feet, 1.8 m) plant has green, lace-like foliage. In Victorian times, Sweet Annie was valued for its apple/cinnamon fragrance, which is so intense that you only have to brush lightly against the plant to release it. Although sweet Annie is an annual, you'll probably never have to re-plant it because the herb self-seeds and spreads prolifically. The Chinese believe sweet Annie to be an antidote for malaria, and it's being tested in America.

Drying

Sweet Annie can be harvested before or after it seeds. The foliage and seeds dry to a lovely golden/reddish brown and the fragrance remains strong. Sweet Annie dries well with both air-drying methods — hanging and screens — and also by pressing.

Crafts

Sweet Annie works well in just about any craft: bouquets, arrangements, garlands, wreaths, potpourris, and swags. Smaller dried sprigs can be hot-glued into wreaths and arrangements, around the rims of hats, and to the outside of sachet bags, while longer lengths can be worked into hearts, circles, and other shapes when fresh-cut. Crafts made from sweet Annie work well in closets, bathrooms, and any other place the fragrance will be enjoyed.

Tansy

Beginning herb gardeners are usually enraptured with tansy because it grows easily just about anywhere. Many experienced herb gardeners, however, view tansy affectionately as a weed because it spreads so prolifically. Tansy leaves look a lot like those of ferns and the herb would make an attractive house plant, but it tends to not do well indoors. Centuries ago tansy leaves were cooked with puddings during the Lent season and the flowers have been used by several cultures to make yellow dye baths.

Drying

Tansy leaves can be harvested at any time and dry best when they are pressed, arranged on a drying rack, or hung upside down in small bundles. The leaves curl slightly as they dry but retain much of their woodsy, artemisia-like fragrance. The bright yellow button blooms should be harvested at their peak and then dropped by their stems through the holes in a screen rack so the blooms dry with support. The blooms are relatively sturdy when dry and retain most of their color and shape.

Crafts

Tansy's feather-like leaves make nice filler, background, and border material for many craft projects. The crushed leaves have traditionally been made into potpourris and sachets because of their reputed ability to repel ants, fleas, and moths. The bright flowers can be used to add a splash of color to hats, wreaths, garlands, potpourris, and ornaments.

Monarda, Chives & Sage

Carnations, Bay
& Lavender

Tarragon

This perennial herb is most appreciated for its culinary contributions. It grows 2 to 3 feet (61 to 91 cm) in height, and likes full sun. (If you have very hot summers, though, partial sun is a better choice.) Russian tarragon, a close relative to the popular French tarragon, is a little too strong for most people's tastes, although it's more winter hardy. The plant spreads slowly but surely, and should be divided every few years.

Drying

Tarragon's dark green foliage deepens in color slightly as it dries, while the greenish-white blooms remain much the same. Dried tarragon leaves curl on the edges, are very brittle, and damage easily, while the blooms and stems remain quite sturdy. Some of tarragon's licorice-like fragrance dissipates as it dries, but you can release the fragrance by just rolling a few dried leaves between your fingers.

The main harvesting should be done in late summer, although it's perfectly okay to harvest a few leaves and blooms earlier in the season. Tarragon can be dried by hanging it upside down in small bundles or on a screen if turned frequently and given lots of space. Tarragon leaves also press well. If you need a few sprigs of tarragon for a craft project, they will dry well in a microwave, but this method absorbs the plant's flavorful oils so it won't work for culinary projects.

Cuisines and Crafts

Tarragon leaves can be used sparingly for a subtle licorice flavor in soups and sauces. The leaves can also be rubbed into meats before cooking for flavorful results. Tarragon is also well known in vinegars and herb butters.

Tarragon makes a nice wreath base. Just arrange the fresh-cut stems around a wire ring and secure by wrapping with thin-gauge wire or monofilament. After the wreath has dried, hot-glue sprigs of your favorite culinary herbs and a few garlic bulbs into the tarragon.

Thyme

Thyme is cultivated and enjoyed today primarily for the culinary pleasures it imparts in a variety of foods. In the mid-1600s, though, it was a common belief that thyme "kills worms in the belly, provokes the terms, and gives safe and speedy delivery to women in labour." (Culpepper's *Color Herbal,* 1649). There are several popular varieties, including creeping, broad leg, French, lemon, and silver thymes. They are all perennials that tend to spread without inhibition, and need little care except an occasional trimming.

Drying

If you plan to use them in a craft project, harvest thyme's blooms, which range in color from white to several shades of pink, at their peak. For culinary projects, the green-and-white or green-and-gray leaves should be harvested before blooming; for craft projects, the leaves can be harvested at any time.

Hang drying tends to produce excellent results, although screen drying can be used for smaller quantities. Thyme presses well and can also be dried in the microwave without silica gel. The blooms hold their shape and color well, although they tend to be a bit delicate; the leaves curl a little but retain much of their marvelous fragrance.

Cuisines and Crafts

Thyme's famous flavor can be enjoyed in soups, sauces, jellies, vinegars, oils, butters, and salt-free herb blends.

Dried creeping thyme makes lovely tussie mussies and small wreaths. The flowers and leaves of other varieties look lovely in wreaths, arrangements, potpourris, garlands, and any other type of project where the fluffy, airy qualities of dried thyme would be appreciated.

Carnations, Bay & Lavender

Roses, Lamb's Ears,
& Scented Geraniums

Yarrow

This well-known perennial is a gardener's dream plant: it attracts bees, spreads easily, needs very little care, and has lovely, colorful blooms. Averaging 1 to 3 feet (30 to 91 cm) in height, yarrow likes full sun and well-drained soil, and can handle a few days without water. The blooms range in color from a creamy white to bright yellow to a red with yellow centers and a pink with white centers. Yarrow has an interesting medicinal history, having been used for toothaches, digestive ails, poultices, and menstrual problems over the centuries.

Drying

The leaves curl some as they dry, but they retain their lovely dark green color. The blooms shrink some and the colors darken a little, but this actually makes them more attractive. The flowers should be harvested at the peak of their bloom, or at least before they begin to turn brown if you can't bear to pick them so soon. Yarrow dries best by simply tying the stems into small bundles and hanging them upside down for a week or two. If you just want to dry the blooms, you can strip off the leaves and drop the stems through a wide-mesh screen rack. The blooms and leaves also press well. The pink varieties do not dry nearly as well as the yellow.

Crafts

Yarrow is a mainstay of herbal crafters because the blooms are large, sturdy, and brightly colored. They work well in wreaths, garlands, swags, basket arrangements, and even in potpourris. Yarrow stems are one of the few herbal stems strong enough to insert directly into a foam, straw, or moss base, and the hollow stems are often slipped over the stems of weaker-stemmed herbs and taped in place.

Index to Common and Botanic Names

Agrimony, *Agrimonia Eupatoria*

Angelica, *Angelica Archangelica*

Anise, *Pimpinella anisum*

Anise Hyssop, *Agastache foeniculum*

Basil, *Ocimum basilicum*

Bay, *Laurus nobilis*

Bee Balm, *Monarda didyma*

Betony, *Stachys officinalis*

Borage, *Borago officinalis*

Broom, *Cytisus scoparius*

Burdock, *Arctium lappa*

Calendula, *Calendula officinalis*

Carnations, *Dianthus caryophyllus*

Catnip, *Nepeta cataria*

Celosia, *Celosia cristata*

Chamomile, *Chamaemelum nobile*

Chervil, *Anthriscus cerefolium*

Chicory, *Cichorium intybus*

Chives, *Allium schoenoprasum*

Comfrey, *Symphytum officinalis*

Coneflower, *Echinacea angustifolia*

Coriander, *Coriandrum sativum*

Dill, *Anethum graveolens*

Dock, *Rumex* spp.

Dusty Miller, *Senecio cineraria*

Elderberry, *Sambucus* spp.

Fennel, *Foeniculum vulgare*

Feverfew, *Chrysanthemum parthenium*

Garlic, *Allium sativum*

Germander, *Teucrium chamaedrys*

Heather, *Calluna vulgarius*

Horehound, *Marrubium vulgare*

Lamb's Ear, *Stachys byzantina*

Lavender, *Lavandula angustifolia*

Lemon Balm, *Melissa officinalis*

Lemon Verbena, *Aloysia triphylla*

Lovage, *Levisticum officinale*

Marjoram, *Origanum majorana*

Mint, *Mentha* spp.

Mugwort, *Artemisia vulgaris*

Parsley, *Petroselinium crispum*

Pennyroyal, *Mentha pulegium*

Queen Anne's Lace, *Daucus carota*

Rose, *Rosaceae*

Rosemary, *Rosmarinus officinalis*

Rue, *Ruta graveolens*

Safflower, *Carthamus tinctorius*

Sage, *Salvia* spp.

Salad Burnet, *Poterium sanguisorba*

Santolina, *Santolina chamaecyparissus*

Scented Geranium, *Pelargonium* spp.

Silver King and Queen Artemisias, *Artemisia ludoviciana*

Sweet Annie, *Artemisia annua*

Tansy, *Tanacetum vulgare*

Tarragon, *Artemisia dracunculus*

Thyme, *Thymus* spp.

Yarrow, *Achillea millefolium*

Index

Bibliography

Bailey, Liberty Hyde. *Encyclopedia of American Horticulture.* New York: MacMillan and Co., 1900.

Bailey, Liberty Hyde and Ethel Zoe. *Hortus Third.* New York: MacMillan Publishing, 1978.

Brickell, Christopher. *The American Horticultural Society Encyclopedia of Garden Plants.* New York: MacMillan Publishing Co., 1989.

Gerard, John. *The Herbal.* New York: Dover Publishing, 1980. (First published in 1633.)

Grieve, Mrs. Maude. *A Modern Herbal.* New York: Harcourt, Brace, and Co., 1931.

Kowalchik and Hilton (Editors). *Rodale's Illustrated Encyclopedia of Herbs.* Emmaus, Pennsylvania: Rodale Press, 1987.

Lovejoy, Sharon. *Sunflower Houses: Garden Discoveries for Children of All Ages.* Loveland, Colorado: Interweave Press, 1991.

Seymour, E.L.D. *The Wise Garden Encyclopedia.* New York: Harper Collins Publishing, revised edition 1990.